View of the construction site, summer 1964
The basement ceiling finished in late September before being concreted over. In the foreground the foundation walls of the ramp with the end wall that would later be demolished; in the background the gondola ropeway for the *First Swiss Garden Show G|59*.

Pavillon Le Corbusier Zurich

Scheidegger & Spiess

PAVILLON LE CORBUSIER ZURICH

Restoration of an Architectural Jewel

City of Zurich, Building Surveyor's Office
Silvio Schmed and Arthur Rüegg

Editors City of Zurich, Building Surveyor's Office,
Silvio Schmed and Arthur Rüegg
Book concept Silvio Schmed and Arthur Rüegg, Zurich
Copy editing Monique Zumbrunn, Zurich
Proofreading Louise Stein, Edinburgh
Book design Robert & Durrer, Zurich

Retouching Peter Habe, Zurich
Lithography Widmer & Fluri GmbH, Zurich
Printing and binding DZA Druckerei zu Altenburg GmbH, Thuringia

Fonts: Neue Helvetica, Stencil
Paper: LuxoArt Samt matte coated 150g/m²

ISBN 978-3-85881-852-2

Verlag Scheidegger & Spiess AG
Niederdorfstrasse 54
8001 Zurich
Switzerland
www.scheidegger-spiess.ch

Scheidegger and Spiess is being supported by the Federal Office of Culture with a general subsidy for the years 2016–2020.

Picture credits
Georg Aerni, Zurich: pp. 8/9, 15, 29, 33, 38/39, 40/41, 42/43, 47, 50 below, 51, 60/61, 62 right, 64, 67, 68, 70, 76 above, 77, 79, 80, 81, 82/83, 88
Archive Fondation Le Corbusier, Paris: pp. 20 below, 27 center, 30 left
Bauen+Wohnen, September 1966, p. 347: p. 30 right
Betty Fleck, Museum für Gestaltung Zurich / ZHdK: pp. 72/73, 74/75
gta Archive, ETH Zurich, Donation Jürg Gasser: pp. 12, 13, 17–19, 21, back endpapers
gta Archive, ETH Zurich, estate of Bernhard Hoesli: front endpapers, pp. 22 center and below, 25, 26 below
gta Archive, ETH Zurich, estate of Heinz Ronner: pp. 23, 24 above, 25, 27 below
Bärbel Högner, Berlin: p. 45
KEYSTONE/PHOTOPRESS-ARCHIVE: p. 11
Stills from the documentary *Centre Le Corbusier. The Last Building of Le Corbusier (1965 –1967)* by Fredi M. Murer and Jürg Gasser: pp. 20 above, 22 above, 24 below, 26 above, 27 above
Museum für Gestaltung Zurich, Graphics Collection: p. 6
Walter and Renate Rohrer, Winterthur: p. 78
Silvio Schmed and Arthur Rüegg, Zurich: pp. 14, 34–37, 44 46, 48, 49, 50 above, 52–59, 62 left, 63, 65, 66, 69, 71, 76 below, 84–87

Heidi Weber welcoming Le Corbusier at Zurich Airport, November 24, 1960
Photo René Burri

With the Pavillon Le Corbusier, the City of Zurich has a truly unique object in its portfolio. This architectural icon, completed in 1967, is situated close to the lakeshore in a spacious park. That Le Corbusier was able to realize this exemplary demonstration of his architectural ideas in such a prime location is thanks solely to the efforts of a risk-taking young gallerist and interior architect, who proved exceptionally adept at translating her visions into reality. Heidi Weber initiated the master's only building in German-speaking Switzerland with unflagging dedication, financed it herself, and together with the architects Alain Tavès and Robert Rebutato saw it through to completion two years after Le Corbusier's death. The City of Zurich had previously granted her a fifty-year lease on the plot between the neo-Gothic Villa Egli and Hermann Haller's studio, which is built entirely of wood. When that lease expired in 2014, title to the pavilion fell to the City, which decided to run it as a Le Corbusier museum that would draw visitors from far and wide to Zurich.

The Building Surveyor's Office of the City of Zurich (AHB) was thereupon entrusted with the full-scale restoration of the structure. The fact that we were dealing with a protected historical monument, which at the time was in desperate need of work to make it fit for purpose as a state-of-the-art exhibition space, made this a somewhat daunting brief. The AHB was therefore fortunate in being able to enlist as architects Silvio Schmed and Arthur Rüegg, two internationally respected, Zurich-based Le Corbusier connoisseurs. Their feasibility study, which was overseen by a *comité scientifique*, identified the pavilion's shell, infrastructure, furnishings, and compatibility with the prevailing standards as the most challenging aspects of the project. Although the structure built entirely of steel and glass had been well-maintained, there could be no doubting the urgent need for action. Between autumn of 2017 and spring of 2019, therefore, the two architects together with the canton's own cultural heritage team and numerous other specialists applied their considerable expertise and eye for detail to the restoration of this jewel. It was a task that more than once called for recourse to unconventional solutions, such as the use of a needle gun to remove the coats of paint covering the intricate steel frame.

The Pavillon Le Corbusier has been open to the public again since May 2019. The City has entrusted its operation to the Museum für Gestaltung Zurich, which has undertaken to stage a new summer exhibition there every year. Now a beautifully preserved historic monument, the pavilion evinces the same freshness, elegance, and color as it had at its opening. That it scarcely looks any different than it did in 1967 may seem paradoxical; yet it also shows how professionally, and with what assiduous attention to detail, the task at hand was solved—not least in the reconstruction of the missing items of furniture and light fixtures. The project was concluded without any faults, moreover, which is certainly not a matter of course; and that in addition to the quality specifications both the budget and schedule were also met is extremely gratifying. The excellent outcome speaks for itself and at the same time attests to the smooth and successful collaboration of all our internal and external experts. It is their work, therefore, that this publication documents and honors. On behalf of the City of Zurich, I would like to extend my sincerest thanks to all those involved for their hard work on this project.

In April 2019, the European Council declared a network of some thirty works by Le Corbusier, among them the Pavillon Le Corbusier in Zurich, to form one of its official "Culture Routes," thus supplying but one reason more to visit this intricate and colorful *tour de force* of Le Corbusier's late period in Zurich.

Wiebke Rösler Häfliger, Director, Building Surveyor's Office of the City of Zurich

Heidi Weber's Exhibition "House"

Arthur Rüegg and Silvio Schmed

Le Corbusier's Zurich pavilion is a demonstration of architectural principles and a laboratory for the synthesis of the arts.

"Synthesis" here means the combination of autonomous but mutually enhancing forms of artistic expression. Such an interaction of architecture, furniture, painting, tapestry, sculpture, and the graphic arts, Le Corbusier argued, is more effectively demonstrated by the "modest and nomadic setting of a dwelling" than by the "arbitrariness commonly found in rooms designed for exhibition purposes."[1] He supplied the framework with which to prove this in the form of an "artist house" assembled out of prefabricated steel and glass elements, whose proportions were derived from the Modulor. Its dual function of private home and exhibition space was of central importance to the client right from the start. The interior designer Heidi Weber, owner of the Galerie Mezzanin, had been Le Corbusier's exclusive art dealer since 1958, and had been instrumental in reissuing the four iconic tubular-steel chairs of 1928/29. As early as 1959, she had dreamed of presenting all the creations of the great artist-architect "in a house that he himself designed."[2]

Weber at first took advantage of the very different spaces to exhibit the works of Le Corbusier himself, turning the spotlight on the history of the pavilion, a series of oil paintings, and finally his buildings for India's new provincial capital of Chandigarh. But in 1969, fearing that the premises might degenerate into a kind of "Le Corbusier Mausoleum,"[3] she had the "Centre Le Corbusier" host an environmental forum with the declared aim of contributing to the "critical engagement with the problems of today's housing and living conditions"[4] in a way that the master himself would have approved of. In the years 1968 to 1977, Weber and her curator, the photographer Jürg Gasser, launched an ambitious program of socially critical shows flanked by talks given by speakers of renown. In September 1968, for example, the pavilion was the scene of a discussion marathon, which has gone down in the annals as the "6-Day-Long Zürcher Manifest." After Gasser's departure in late 1977, the Gottlieb Duttweiler Institute with its Corbusier Community Workshop (CoCo) moved in on a two-year lease, which was not, however, renewed. The pavilion thereafter remained closed, as it had been from 1973 to 1976,[5] and not until 1984 did it once again offer new insights into the work of the *homo universalis* Le Corbusier.

Weber had always reserved the rough-plastered basement of the pavilion for Le Corbusier's own works of art—even during CoCo's interregnum. While she presented his drawings and gouaches under glass in box-like oak frames, Gasser worked on developing modular support systems for the two upper stories based on the steel-frame modules. Over the years, many of the oak plywood façade panels were doubled up with chipboard panels painted in various colors until certain parts of the building—the two-story studio, for example—had been completely remodeled.

After the "Heidi Weber Haus von Le Corbusier" passed to the City of Zurich in 2014, Cultural Affairs staged four summer exhibitions there, notwithstanding the very difficult climatic conditions that by then were prevailing in the basement. Since the conclusion of the restoration work, the pavilion has been run as a public museum by the Museum für Gestaltung Zurich. There are good grounds to hope that it will become a living cultural center in which the younger generation can re-evaluate the synthesis of architecture, art, and life championed by Le Corbusier.

Das letzte Gebäude von Le Corbusier, Einweihung und Eröffnung, from July 15, 1967 at the “Centre Le Corbusier.” Exhibition of photos, sketches, plans, models, furniture, and lithographs.

The end wall of the studio with Jürg Gasser’s three photo panels on the construction of the pavilion and a graphic representation of the Modulor scale (right).

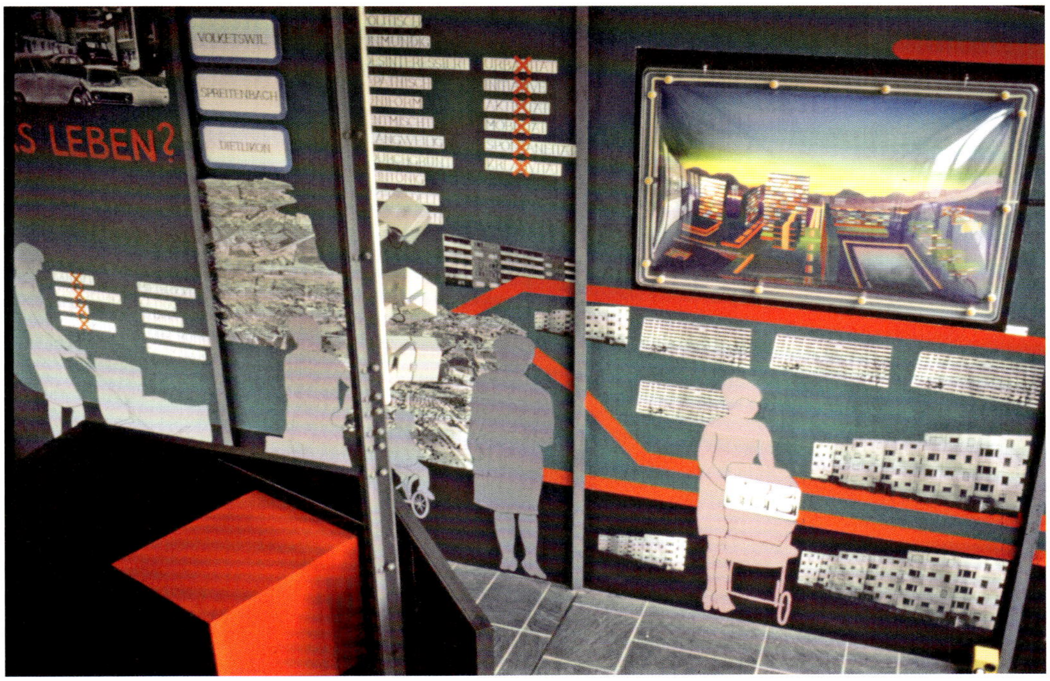

Kinder sehen ihre Siedlung. Zeichenwettbewerb des Städtebauinstituts Nürnberg, August 23 to mid-November, 1969 at the "Centre Le Corbusier – Forum für Umweltsfragen."

Exhibition of children's drawings from a sociological experiment by Professor Gerhard G. Dittrich, shown in exchange for Jürg Gasser's Chandigarh exhibition.

Zürich? Diagnose und Therapie für eine Stadt. Eine Ausstellung der Studiengruppe "Bauen für Zeitgenossen," February 26 to May 1970 at the "Centre Le Corbusier – Forum für Umweltsfragen."

At top right a skylight dome painting by Max Matter. Curated by a multidisciplinary group led by Leonhard Fünfschilling and Hermann Huber together with Jürg Gasser.

Chandigarh sehen. Schweizer Reportagen, May 21–October 4, 2015 at the "Centre Le Corbusier—Museum Heidi Weber" (City of Zurich Cultural Affairs)

Photography exhibition with a central mosaic of photos from Jürg Gasser's Chandigarh show of 1968. A joint project with the Institute for the History and Theory of Architecture (gta) at ETH Zurich curated by Bruno Maurer and Arthur Rüegg with scenography by Silvio Schmed.

Mon univers, May 11–November 17, 2019 at the "Pavillon Le Corbusier" (Museum für Gestaltung Zurich)

In the basement: originals from Le Corbusier's private collection; in the studio: a partial reconstruction, using replicas, of the exhibition *L'art dit primitif dans la maison d'aujourd'hui* (1935); in the upper story: large-format exhibits from the worlds of art, industry, folk art, and nature. Curated by Christian Brändle and Arthur Rüegg with scenography by Silvio Schmed.

The Realization of a Manifesto

Arthur Rüegg and Silvio Schmed

A free-standing, sheltering roof and underneath it an independent spatial complex—that was the concept behind Le Corbusier's ideal exhibition receptacle.

In 1950 Le Corbusier proposed erecting a monumental *parapluie-parasol* at the Porte Maillot in Paris. It was to consist of two adjoining squares, underneath which an artist group would be able to exhibit its works to the public. Iconic steel canopies defining a public space were also the starting point for the design of the Zurich pavilion in 1960. Instead of an open-air exhibition space, however, Le Corbusier now envisioned a prototypical residential building, which, having been conceived initially in concrete, was ultimately realized as a "loose system of colored building blocks"[1] in a demonstratively prefabricated, visibly bolted-together steel frame.

Construction began as early as the spring of 1964. Even before the details of the design had been finalized, site architect Willy Boesiger of Zurich had the double-shell basement cast in concrete—a later addition that was not part of the original program. Le Corbusier approved the plans for the canopy roof in July 1965. This 40-tonne structure, for the most part welded together out of 5- and 6-mm-thick sheet steel, rests on three tubular-steel posts and six box posts with a rectangular cross section.[2] Each of the two squares, which are linked by a connecting piece, is made up of four planes tilted toward each other to form a saddle-like figure and then reinforced by welded-on diagonal ribs. The elements, which were built by the firm of Wartmann in Brugg in the winter of 1965/66, were assembled on site and hoisted into place by a pneumatic crane.

The assembly of the *corps de logis* commenced only after the topping-out on May 25, 1966. Its construction rests on a system for the serial manufacture of holiday homes, which Le Corbusier had patented in 1950 and with the help of the engineers Louis Fruitet and Jean Prouvé brought to fruition for the Zurich pavilion. The supporting structure comprises frames made of angle profiles that are joined together to form cubes with 2.26-m-long sides—a standard length derived from the Modulor. These were assembled on the concrete basement with the aid of no fewer than 22,000 bolts. The glass panels, enameled sheet metal, wall and ceiling elements were inserted into this Cartesian framework. The exchangeability of all the components was a crucial part of the program.

Boesiger resigned on February 5, 1966, just a few months after Le Corbusier's death. After a two-month lull, Alain Tavès and Robert Rebutato—two Atelier 35-S architects of many years' standing—took over the planning and site management. They drew a set of some 160 detailed execution plans and solved the remaining problems afflicting the assembly, infrastructure, color scheme, and furnishings; they also found a way of providing the basement with natural light. Le Corbusier had enlisted his trusted enameller, Jean Martin, to develop the plates of enameled sheet metal, whose execution was entrusted to a firm that specialized in large formats, Boos & Hahn of Ortenberg, Germany. The neoprene profile for fixing the composite glass panels in place, drawn by Serge Binotto of the Atelier Prouvé, turned out to be unusable and the prototype supplied had to be replaced by a wider model with two lock strips.[3] The pavilion is also a textbook case of the difficulty of integrating installation systems in industrially organized buildings.[4] After a seven-year planning and construction period, Heidi Weber was able to ceremoniously inaugurate the programmatic exhibition building on July 15, 1967.

Provisional assembly of the prefabricated roof elements at Wartmann & Co., Brugg, winter 1965/66.

On the construction site, spring 1966
Once on site, the roof elements delivered by an oversize-load vehicle were jacked up and then welded together. The box posts were righted and provisionally fixed. Here the west canopy has already been raised by a pneumatic crane; the central round post is still missing.

View of the construction site, spring 1966
The west canopy suspended from the pneumatic crane. The foundation walls are all that is visible of the ramp; the end wall has been demolished to allow the ramp to be extended. In the background the gondola ropeway of the *First Swiss Garden Show G|59* shortly before dismantling.

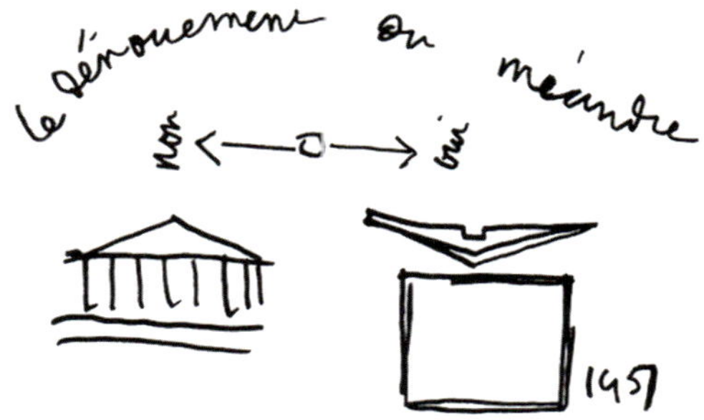

The pavilion's *parapluie-parasol* marries the traditional gable roof and the "modern" butterfly roof in a single structure. Their relationship is a dialectical one, as is that of the upward and downward tilting roof canopies. Drawing from Le Corbusier, *Entre-deux ou propos toujours reliés*, Paris: Editions Forces-Vives, 1970, final image (detail).

Topping-out ceremony under the canopies, now firmly in place, May 25, 1966
The *G|59* gondola ropeway has already gone.

Porte Maillot, Project B, 1950. Photomontage of the model (FLC 18154) whose graphic canopies were a starting point for the Zurich project.

View of the construction site, winter 1966/67
The prefabricated steel frame complete with ventilation flaps has been assembled underneath the canopies. On the right the scaffolding for the installation of the enameled panels. The glass panels are still missing. The double-shell concrete ramp, insulated with foam panels, has already been cast.

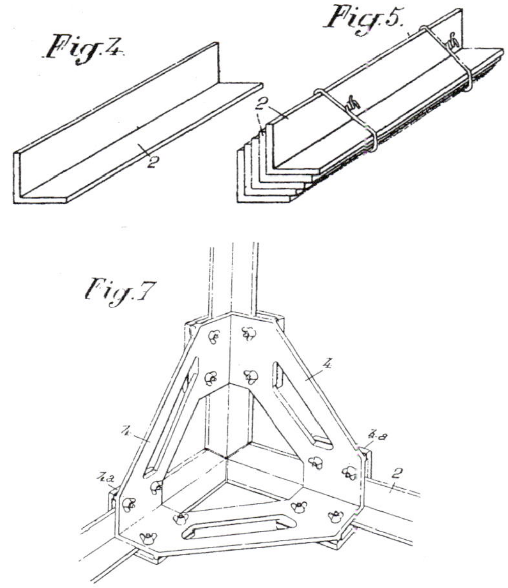

Angle profiles, 2.26 m in length, as per the Modulor. Profile packing with assembly tool to facilitate welding into three-dimensional units, which were to have been assembled on site. Drawing from patent application No. 1.029.744 of December 15, 1950 (detail)

Angle profiles being welded together into square steel frames at Wartmann in Brugg, summer 1966.

Assembly of the steel frames on the construction site, summer 1966
The leveling was done with the aid of metal plates on cement plinths (as per the drawing of July 19, 1966). Bolted together with separate spacers, the two-dimensional frames form a perfectly orthogonal, cubic grid.

Finished steel frame with infill and with welded-on connector plates, whose joints are left open. The tar paper insulating the perimeter has become stuck to the bottom edge of the plates.

Trial assembly of steel frames and floor plates on the construction site, summer 1966
The final assembly was done floor by floor (see photograph on endpapers).

The wiring runs through horizontal and vertical ducts made of plastic or metal. At the bends, however, the cables are left exposed, meaning that after cementing the wiring can no longer be replaced or the ducts used for additional lines.

Iron pipes with regulating valves for the underfloor heating on the ground floor. Welded-on fixture for the ventilation of the underfloor heating system.

Inside view of the metal frame at ground-floor level, autumn 1966
The ground-floor underfloor heating was laid under the steel frame and covered with sand and clay tiles. This was then topped with a layer of lean concrete and then the slate flagstones in a bed of mortar.

Enameled panels after firing at Boos & Hahn in Ortenberg, Germany, autumn 1966
Spray painting made for a very even coating.

Enameled panels from the inside after installation, winter 1966/67
The sheet metal panels were first lined with plaster to stabilize them and insulated with mineral wool. Each panel was then sealed off with an inside vapor barrier. Finally, the oak plywood cladding was screwed onto the frame.

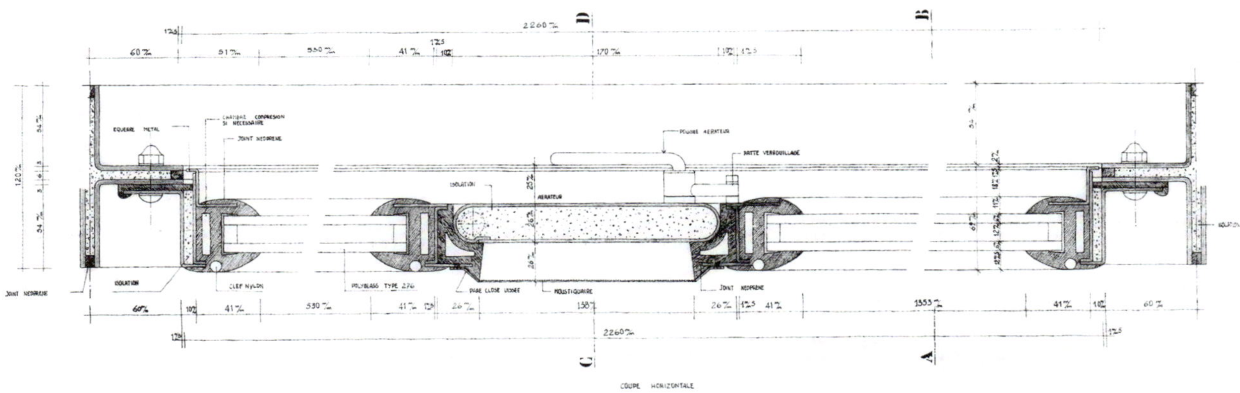

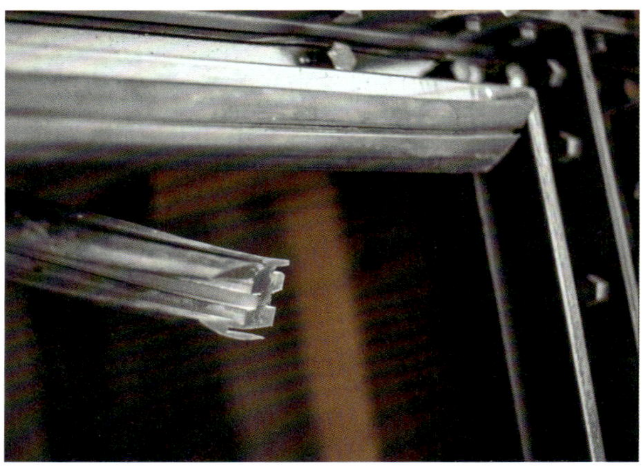

Insertion of the composite glass panels into the steel frame of the façade, spring 1967.
The vulcanized neoprene seals are mitered together in the corners.

Horizontal section through a façade unit with composite glass and ventilation flap
The execution plan of June 8, 1966 drawn up by Tavès and Rebutato shows the first neoprene profile with only one lock strip cavity, which proved unusable in practice.

Le Corbusier's Last Work

Roger Strub

The exhibition pavilion on the Zürichhorn is Le Corbusier's only building in German-speaking Switzerland and the last of his ready-to-build projects to be seen through to completion. When the pavilion fell to the City of Zurich, it was placed under cantonal and federal protection and restored in accordance with the regulations governing the preservation of historical monuments.

The building opened only in 1967. The fact that the architect himself had died two years previously in the summer of 1965 engendered a certain insecurity among the architectural critics of the day, who were unsure how to characterize it: Could the posthumously completed pavilion be considered a genuine Le Corbusier at all? Did the exhibition space erected in the mid-1960s accord with the contemporary understanding of architecture? And later on, another question emerged: Was this really a historical monument?

From today's perspective, Le Corbusier's authorship is undisputed. Catherine Dumont d'Ayot, working under Professor Uta Hassler at the Institute of Construction History and Preservation at ETH Zurich, has studied the history of how the pavilion came about in considerable depth.[1] Her findings show just how intensive and specific Le Corbusier's involvement in this building project was. All the really crucial planning decisions were made by Le Corbusier himself in dialogue with his client, Heidi Weber. His involvement in the project was wide-ranging, moreover, extending from its conceptualization, which in many respects constituted a continuation of earlier studies, to the formulation of concrete aspects of the construction. One special focus of his work lay on the connecting principles for the steel frame elements, since the system's modularity and flexibility were to be articulated in the intelligibility of its individual parts—even after those parts had been joined together to form a whole. Le Corbusier therefore insisted that the parts should be visibly bolted together and fiercely resisted the contractor's preference for welding as a means of simplifying the assembly process.

Whether the pavilion constituted an important testimony to the contemporary understanding of architecture even at the time of its building can remain a moot point, since its significance as a monument and to the history of architecture is, in fact, related rather to its position in Le Corbusier's oeuvre. As the last of his works to be built, the Zurich pavilion is powerful testimony to the development of his work as a whole and undoubtedly counts as a monument in its own right. The design grew out of the architect's past and present reflections on exhibition spaces in general as well as the idea formulated by Heidi Weber of summarizing his life's work—the architectural designs, the theories of dwelling and building, and his works of art—in *one* place, didactically arranged under *one* roof. At the same time, with its turn to steel-frame construction, the pavilion signals a remarkable new departure in Le Corbusier's work.

His choice of this method was born of the notion of variability. In contrast to the fixed, smoothly joined, chromatically neutral roof, which besides marking the site also provides shelter from sun and rain, the autonomous spatial constellation installed underneath it was to form a *contrepart*—so Le Corbusier's intent—by conveying both mobility and versatility; hence the importance of assembling it so that it could be adapted and even dismantled, at least in theory. That the possibility of dismantling was no more than an intellectual conceit is evident from the fact that Le Corbusier did not object to the addition of a basement. The pavilion's eventual disassembly was never seriously discussed, and no one these days would want to see it disappear—fortunately.

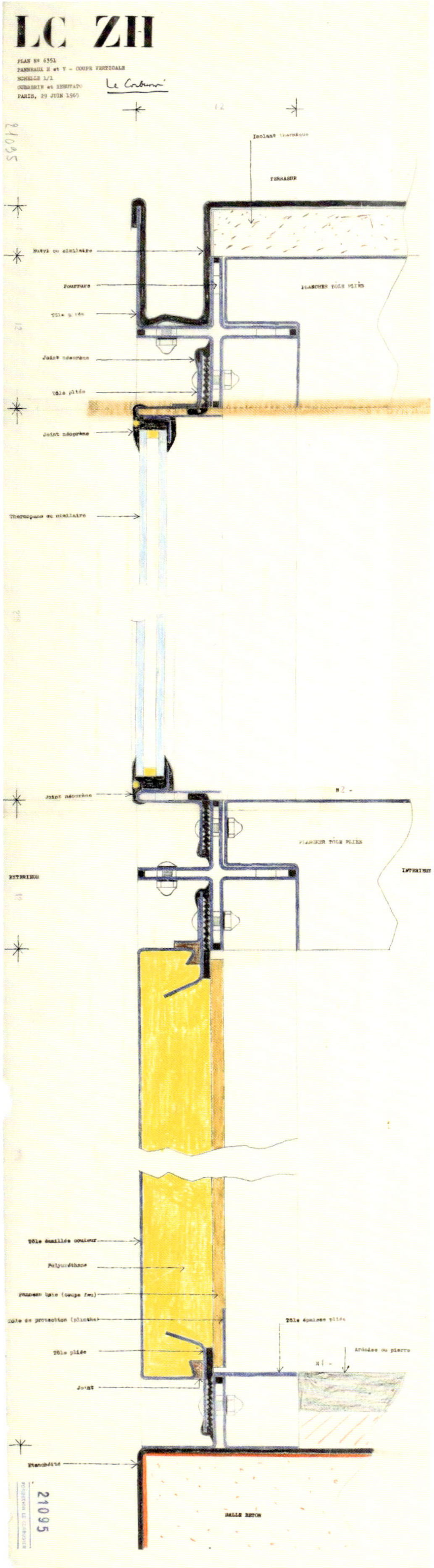

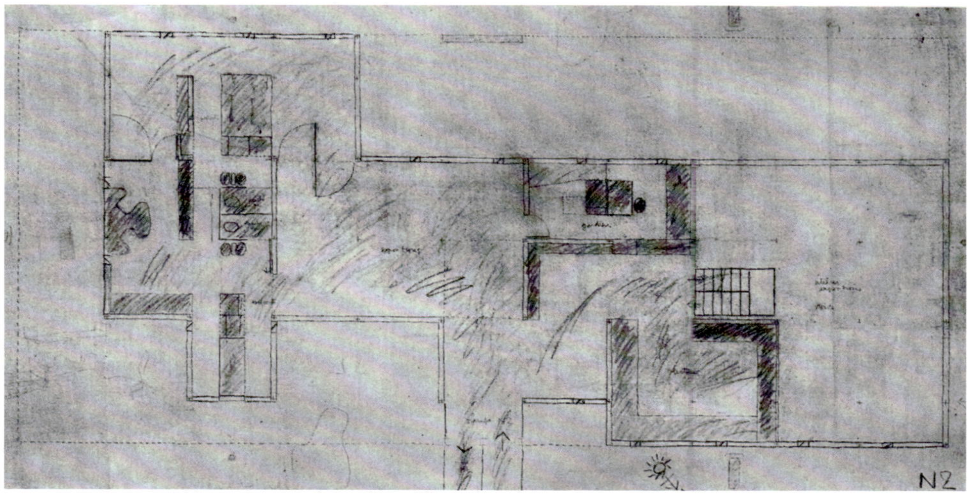

Plans of levels N1 and N2 (ground floor and upper story) on a scale of 1:20 of April 7, 1964, with studio stamp (whereabouts of the originals unknown)
These large-scale plans feature details—probably in Le Corbusier's own hand—of the dimensions, functions, and installations, as well as circulation inside the building. The bedrooms originally intended for the upper story can still be made out, while in most other respects, the layout matches what was actually built.

Façade section on a scale of 1:1 of June 29, 1965, drawn by José Oubrerie and Robert Rebutato and signed by Le Corbusier (Atelier no. 6351, FLC 21095)
This section with details of the dimensions and materials belongs to a set of execution plans that Le Corbusier validated shortly before his death.

The City of Zurich, as the owner of the property, is bound by law to preserve it undiminished, like all its protected historical monuments.[2] At the behest of the pavilion's previous owner, who was also the client who commissioned it, the Building Department of the Canton of Zurich in 2014 declared both the pavilion itself and its landscaped grounds to be part of Zurich's cultural heritage and hence deserving of protection. Since the pavilion is a building whose importance extends far beyond Zurich, both the cantonal department for the preservation of historical monuments and the federal government agreed to help finance its restoration, subject to the proviso that it be placed under federal protection, which for the City of Zurich resulted in a partial loss of title in favor of the Swiss Confederation.

Conserving such an intricate building, in which every detail is the result of a deliberate design decision, is a very demanding undertaking. The ultimate aim of all protective measures and of all restoration work is to conserve a building in such a state that both now and in the future it may serve as testimony—testimony to a different period, to different notions of design, to different social circumstances and technical possibilities, testimony to intentions and convictions, testimony to architectural developments.

The otherness of historical buildings, irrespective of whether they date from recent times or from the distant past, is an enrichment of our world and a daily source of inspiration—especially when the building in question stands in a prominent public location, as does the pavilion. Otherness is undoubtedly one quality that the Pavillon Le Corbusier possesses in abundance: It is a building whose roof and corpus are completely separate from each other; it is a "house" in which notions of dwelling merge with those of a museum. As a pavilion, a typology we always think of as being airy and lightweight, it seems unusually detached from its larger architectural context—standing, as it does, diagonally to the street and the neighboring Villa Egli and Hermann Haller's studio. In fact it is oriented to the trajectory of the sun and the sense of wellbeing we derive from sunlight—hence Le Corbusier's name for it: *Maison d'homme*.

The building's power as testimony, however, dwells not in its external form or appearance alone, for all their extraordinary potency. It resides first and foremost in its material substance. It matters that the neoprene window seals have been preserved (albeit not everywhere) and that the wood veneer of the built-in fittings is the same as when the pavilion was first built. For only the historical material substance can support the full information load of this work, and with it its full value as testimony; only the material substance can serve as a primary historical source for the future.

The desire to preserve a building's substance always sits uncomfortably with the perceived value of allowing a quasi-natural aging process—that is to say, acknowledging its transience. Whereas the durability of the enameled surfaces of the wall panels and that of the slate flagstones seems to know no bounds, the bolted-together steel sections were beginning to rust, the rubber seals had become brittle, and the glass cloudy. Wrestling with these contradictions is a large part of what conservation work is all about. Numerous conflicting wishes and considerations therefore had to be weighed up prior to the restoration of the Pavillon Le Corbusier.

It is Heidi Weber we have to thank for the fact that the pavilion stands in Zurich, that Le Corbusier agreed to build it here notwithstanding his ambivalence about Switzerland, and that the pavilion still stands today; but we can also be grateful that the City of Zurich, as the new owner, has continued to take such good care of it. It has acknowledged, for example, that this spindly building cannot be used at will. It is the pavilion itself that will dictate its use, not vice versa. The City therefore formulated the potential uses accordingly and only then launched its search for a new operator that would understand them.

Finally, the two architects it selected to oversee the pavilion's restoration are both locals with an impressive track record of handling historically significant buildings: Silvio Schmed, an architect who is as assiduous in his analysis as in his execution, and Arthur Rüegg, who counts among the world's leading experts in the work of Le Corbusier.

Restoration, Reconstruction, Retrofitting

Arthur Rüegg and Silvio Schmed

Although the pavilion was well-maintained over a period of many years, the feasibility study overseen by an international team of experts in 2015 revealed an urgent need for action.

First, the shell of the building was no longer watertight—neither the double concrete shell sunk into the groundwater and the ramp corpus nor the neoprene seals holding the composite glass panels in place in the upper stories. The coats of paint on the steel canopy, moreover, had turned out to be laden with pollutants. Second, the infrastructure was severely damaged: The convectors and underfloor heating had been out of order since 1982; a small fire had wreaked havoc with the switch cabinet; and most of the built-in light fixtures had corroded and were no longer working. Third, the pavilion fell woefully short of today's building standards in numerous respects. And finally, many of the fittings and furnishings were missing, among them the tiered seating for spectators in the basement and the lighting designed by Le Corbusier himself.

Apart from this list of faults, however, the pavilion had been preserved practically in its original condition. For once, it was easy to place the preservation and conservation of the material substance of the building, complete with all the signs of wear, at the heart of the restoration concept—all the more so since there was to be no repurposing that might have necessitated compliance with today's norms. As always, however, the fundamental objective had to be weighed up against numerous peripheral factors. The wheelchair access ramp to both Haller's studio and the pavilion planned as part of the project to remodel the lower Höschgasse, for example, was realized in such a way that it accorded with Le Corbusier's original concept.

The color of paint to be used for the steel canopy—for which there were no original findings—and the steel frame of the *corps de logis* was likewise selected with painstaking attention to detail. While the enameled panels required only minor retouching, the majority of the composite glass panels had to be replaced; that being the case, it was decided that sun protection glass should take the place of the adhesive sun control film hitherto used on the south façade. The replacement of the neoprene seals with silicone seals entailed trial and error, nor was the glazing technique easy to master. The original cork insulation on the roof could be left in situ, whereas the severely rusted sheet-metal connectors—as everywhere else on the building—could be salvaged only after the arduous and finicky task of welding in extra plates.

In contrast to the outside coats of paint, the original paintwork on the inside of the pavilion had survived, complete with many of the built-in fixtures. The preserved paintwork was merely retouched and the varnishing refreshed. As in 1967, the spatial impression we have of the pavilion today is shaped largely by the exposed oak façade panels. It was decided that no attempt would be made to improve the energy ratings. Absolutely essential, however, was the installation of proper underfloor heating and a dehumidifier in the basement exhibition space, as only then could the climatic problems afflicting that space be overcome as a necessary precondition to its future use. Fortunately, the original slate flagstones could be saved and relaid. None of the experts consulted queried the decision to install replicas of the missing furnishings, fittings, and light fixtures—including the small spotlights—which thanks to the extremely exact measurements previously taken could be reconstructed with the utmost precision, making them all but impossible to tell apart from the originals.[1] The replicas are discreetly identified as such, but the surface tinged to match the originals. So the pavilion now once again comes across as a credible whole—as complete and radiantly fresh as when it was first built.

Site measurement plans by Schmed/Rüegg, 2018

West façade

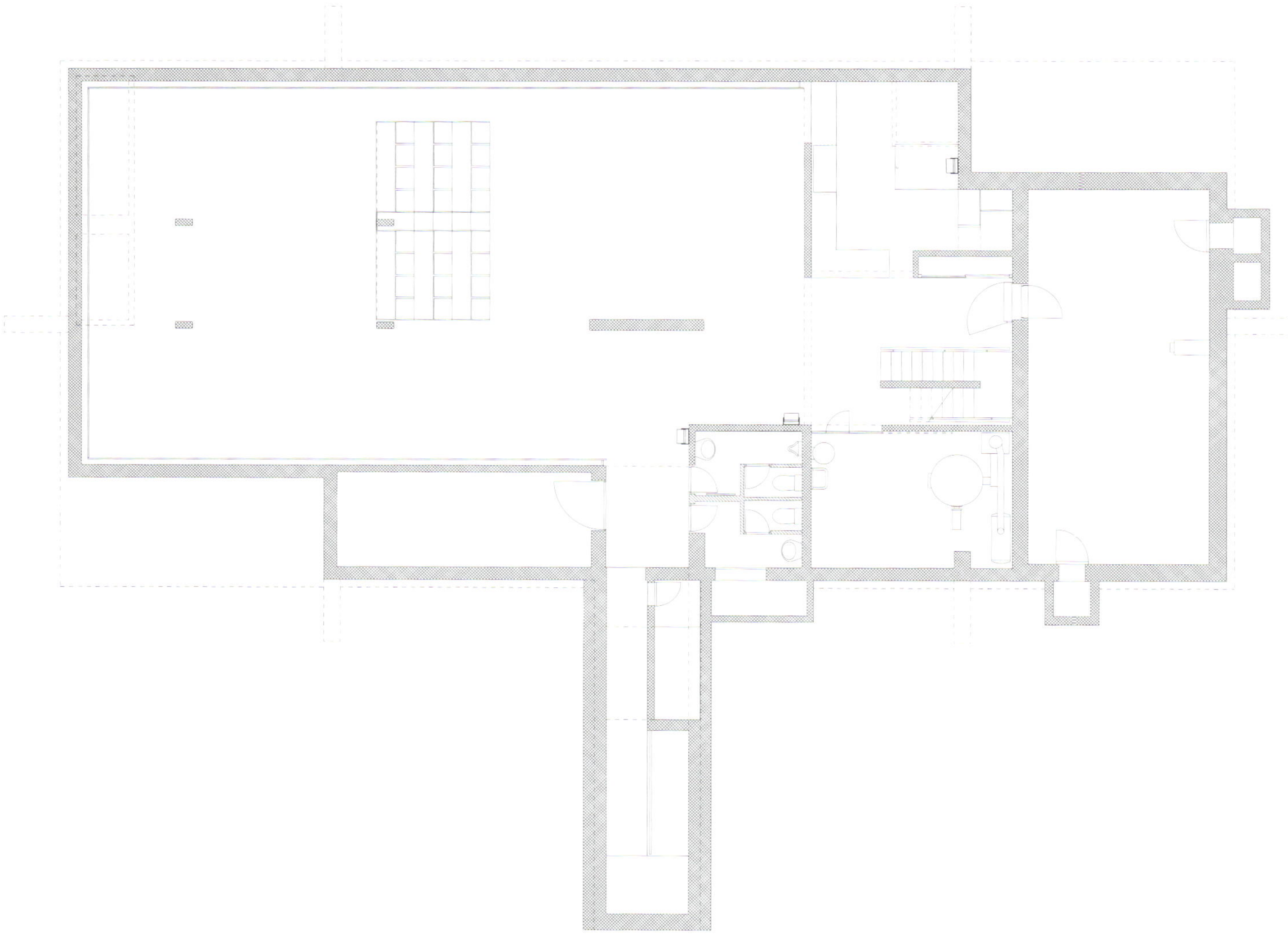

Basement

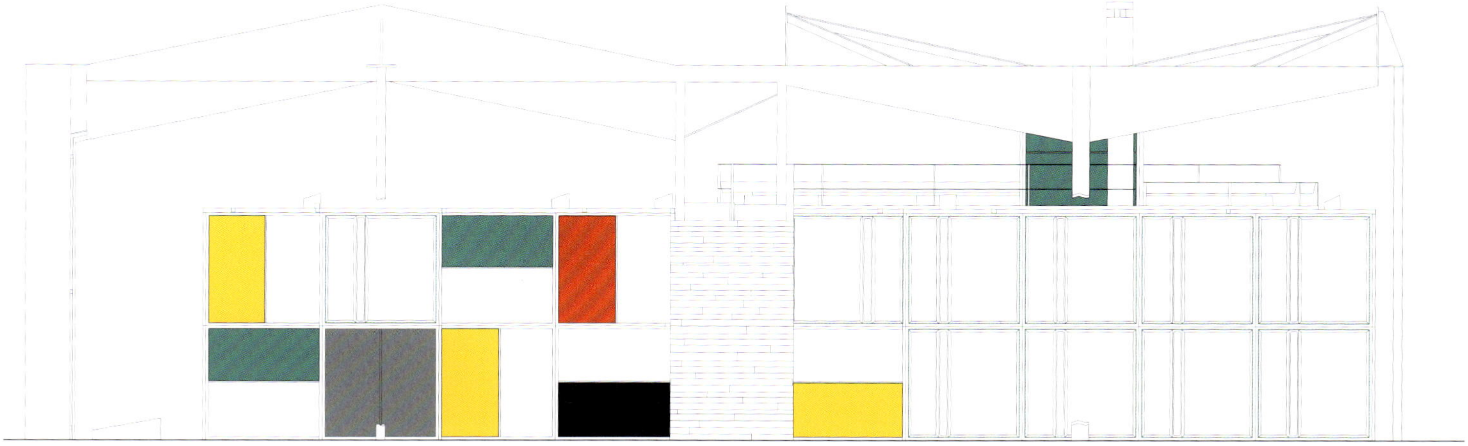

North façade

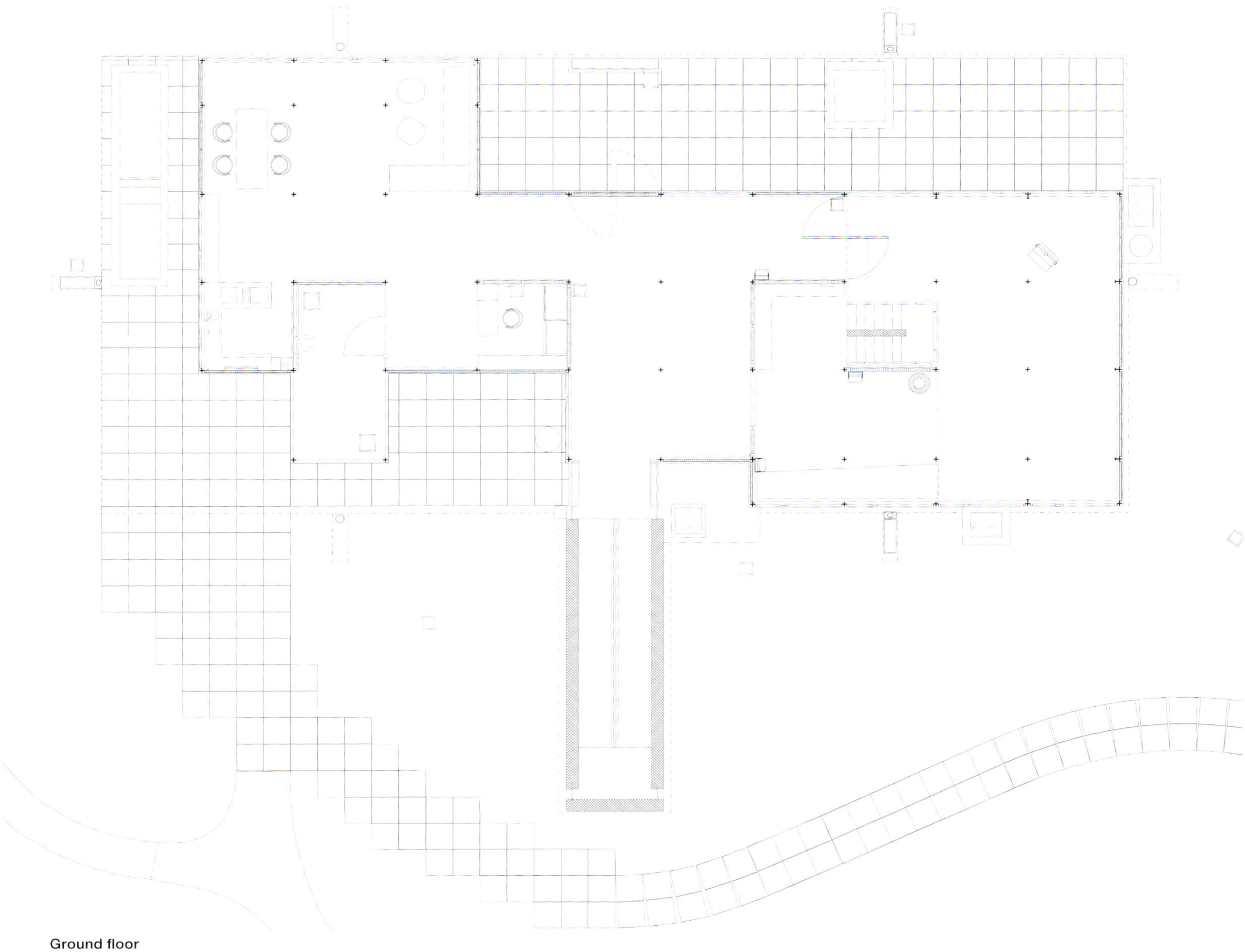

Ground floor

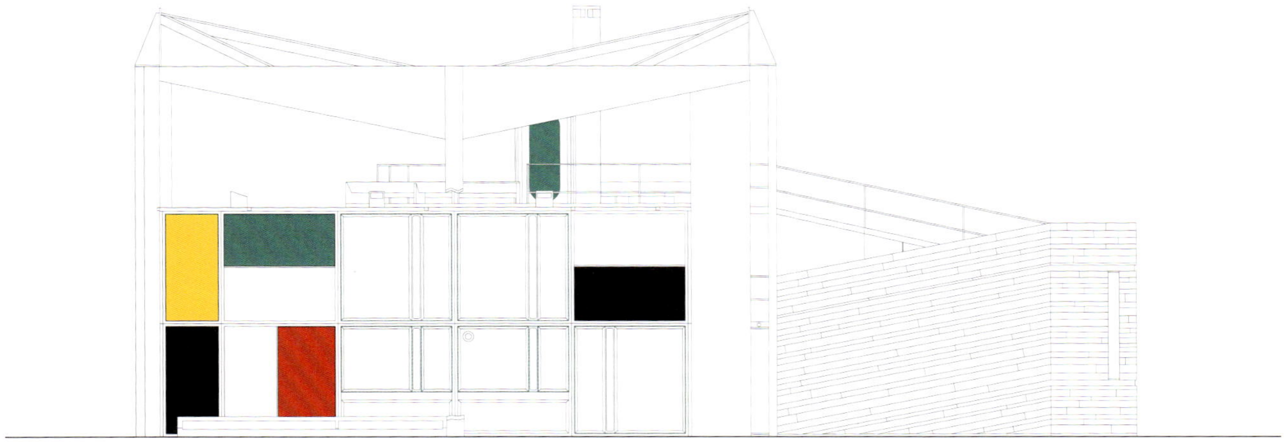

East façade

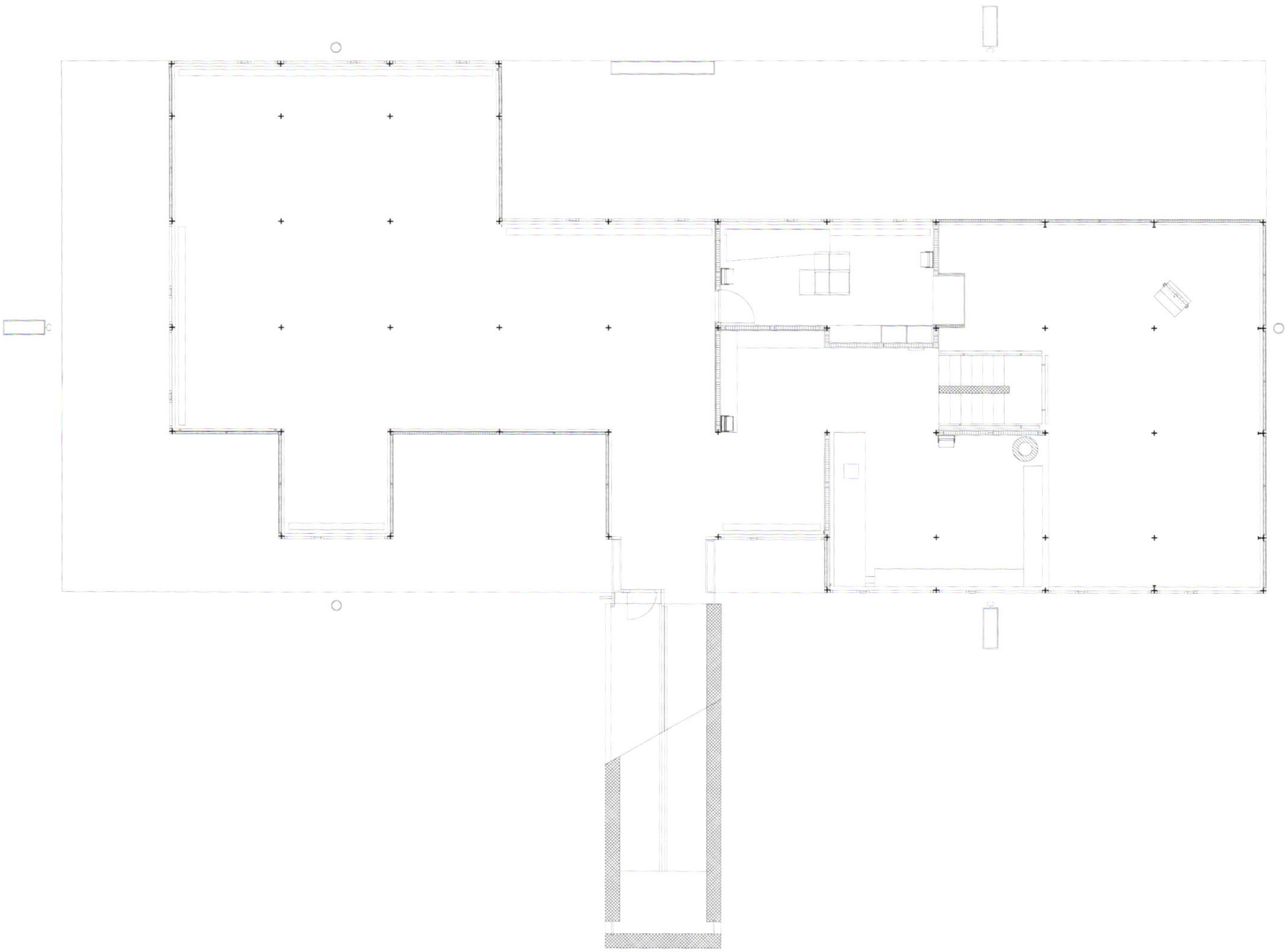

Upper story

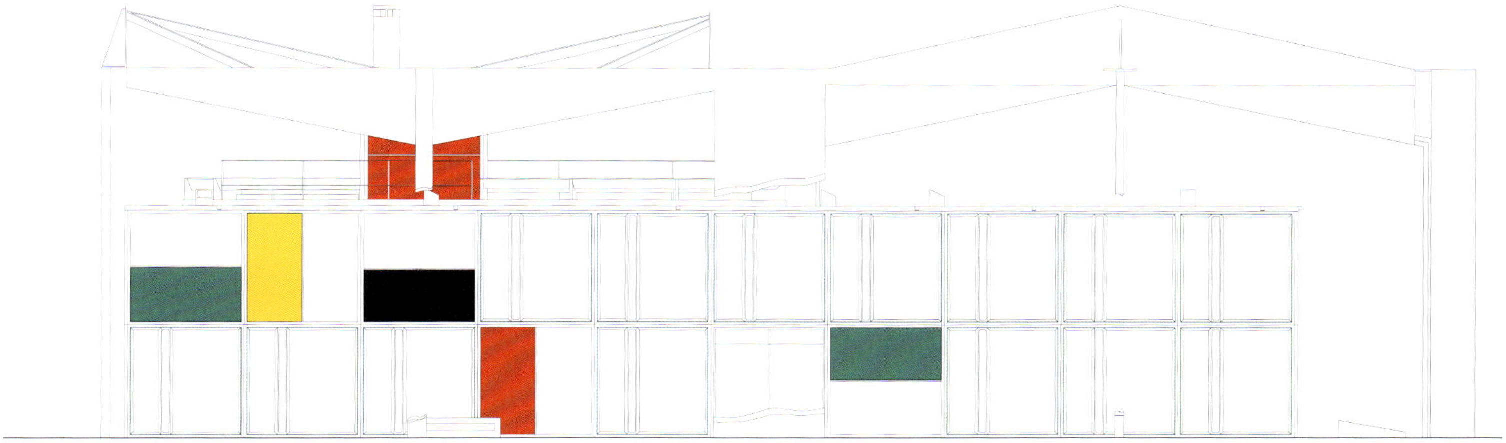

South façade

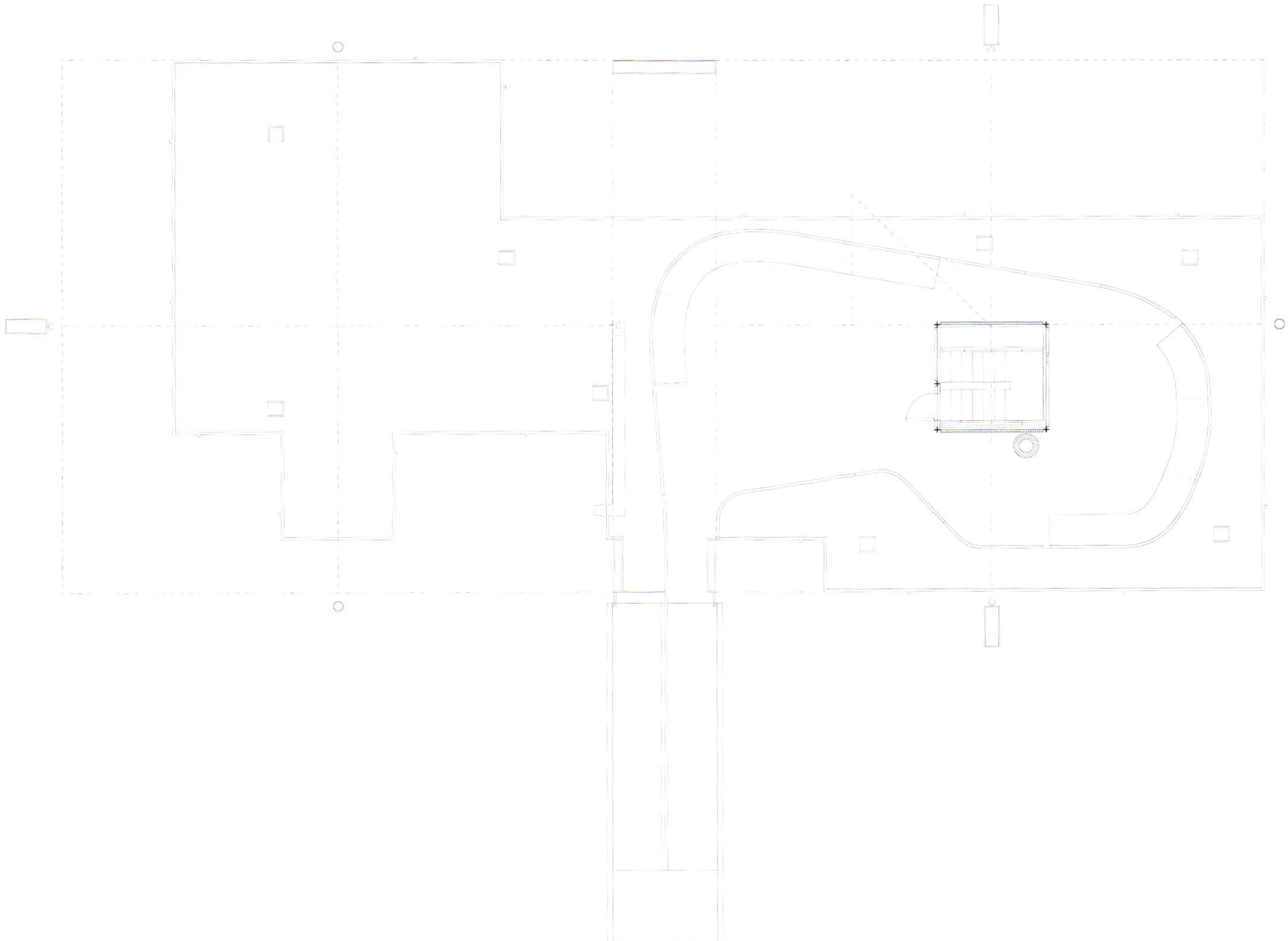

Rooftop

The restoration work called for three sets of scaffolding: one outside the building to support the temporary roof, one on the façade, which was erected on the projecting basement story, and finally a special housing enclosing the canopies, which served as a vacuum chamber for the decontamination work. Only after this housing had been dismantled could the renovation of the roof skin commence.

Sandblasting was used to remove the PCB-contaminated paint coating the top of the canopies. Inside the vacuum chamber the workers had to wear special suits with their own oxygen supply.

The new corrosion protection consists of three layers: a primer, an intermediate coat, and a top coat. These can be applied only at an ambient temperature over 10° Celsius and a relative humidity of below 70 percent; hence their application inside the housing. The thickness of each coat was measured, checked, and recorded. After priming, the undercoat and finish coat were applied in the color of those original elements that had been preserved.

Rooftop terrace after restoration, 2019
The cork insulation on the flat rooftop complete with the bitumen used to seal it were salvaged. Only at the edge of the roof was it removed to enable the installation of new guttering in the existing channels. The entire rooftop was then sealed with two layers of bitumen. The areas outside the terrace were covered with protective foil and washed round gravel in the original grain size. The terrace with its glued-on Pirelli Studway flooring turned out to be rather more complex, as the building physics required the insertion of a vapor control layer underneath the new coat of mortar.

Partly hidden by the old coats of paint: patches of rust on the connector plates.

The dismantled railing on the rooftop terrace
The sheet metal base was cut open, the railing dismantled, the stumps sealed with bitumen and liquid plastic to prevent further corrosion, and the railing then reinstalled. Only then were the openings rewelded to seal them.

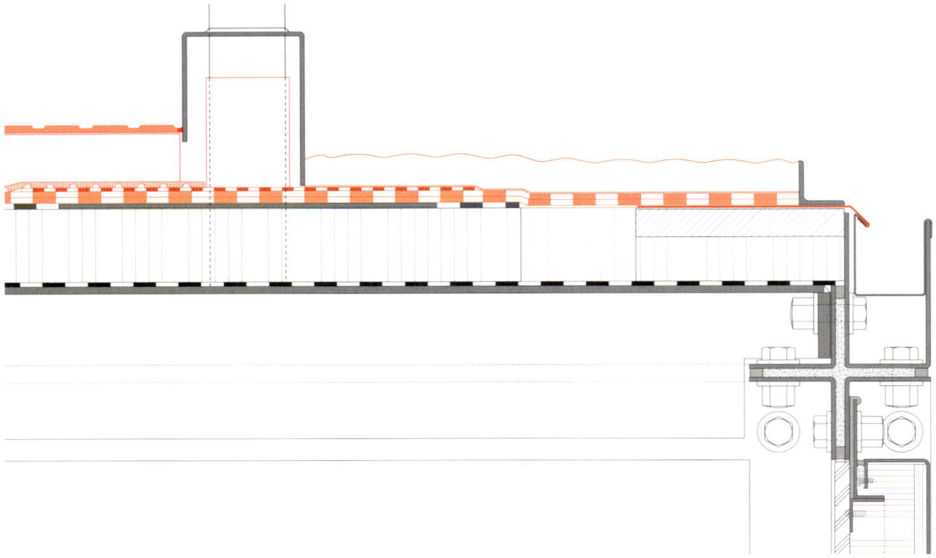

Section through the edge of the roof; on the left the railing of the rooftop terrace.

The rooftop terrace after restoration, 2019
Reconstruction of the corroded dilatation box.

Reconstruction of the original guttering profile in the original dimensions on the flat roof.

Severely rusted ground floor ventilation flaps with fly screen, before and after repair.

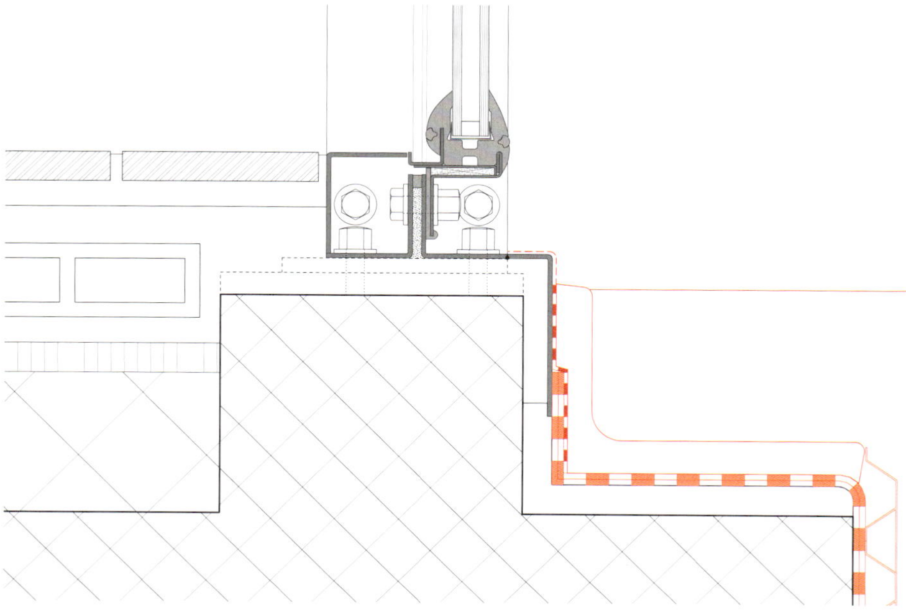

Section through the floor of the ground floor at ground level

In 1967, angled metal plates were welded onto the steel frame at its transition to the bare earth, their function being to connect to the perimeter insulation. This ran counter to the whole concept, however, as it meant the frame could no longer be dismantled. The joints between the connector plates were left open, moreover, which led to extensive rusting owing to the water that seeped in.
All the parts that had rusted through were carefully cut out and replaced with new plates. In order not to destroy the existing rubber seals holding the windows and enameled panels in place, gas-shielded welding was used for this task, and then only at short intervals so that the plates could cool off again.

The work on the steel frame brought to light patches of rust that had not been apparent at first. Once the panes of glass had been removed and the rebates exposed, numerous instances of corrosion were discovered, ranging from patches of rust to the disintegration of entire steel profiles. Here is a glass rebate plate at the bottom of a frame being replaced.

Not all of the angle profiles of the steel frame were hot galvanized prior to assembly. In many instances, "white rust" had formed underneath the coats of paint, rendering any repainting impossible. Contrary to what had originally been assumed, therefore, the profiles with contact to the outside had to be completely stripped. To save the rubber seals inserted between the frame and the composite glass and enameled panels at the time of building, the layers of paint were removed mechanically with the aid of a pneumatic needle gun. After this very arduous process, the bare sheet metal was treated with three coats of corrosion protection paint and finally a double coat of gray paint, as found.

The replica profiles are made of silicone, which these days is the standard material for use in rolling stock and motor vehicles. They are supposed to have a lifespan of at least 25 years. Several versions were made and put through their paces. The minimal improvements are barely visible, but influence important aspects. Their design allows the insulation glass to be deeply embedded inside the silicone profile with the inner and outer lip at the same height after glazing. To ensure that any water that might seep in can run off, the layered metal plates on the bottom rebate were sealed with putty. In addition, the lower parts of the frame were fitted with several blind rivet nuts so that the water could run off.

The original glazing complete with seals on the east side of the pavilion, parts of the north façade, and the roof structure could be preserved, whereas the whole of the south side was reglazed with new sun protection glass. The photo shows the silicone window seals cut to size prior to glazing.

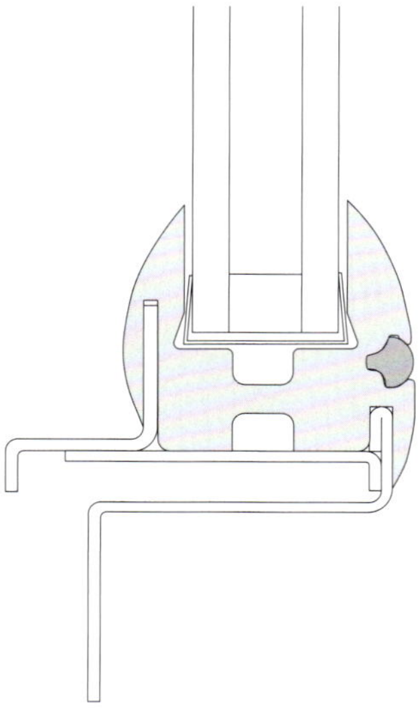

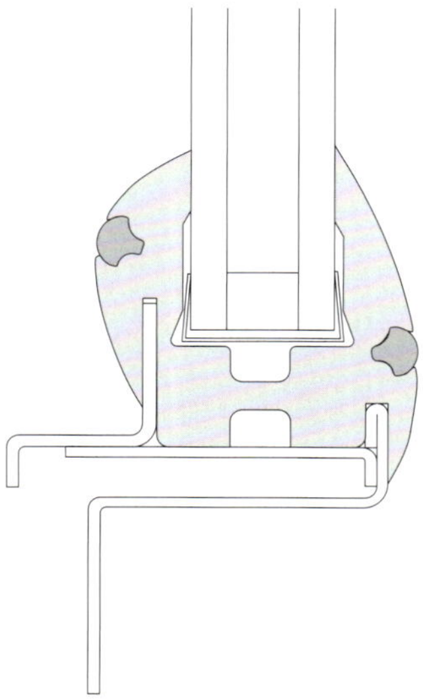

Neoprene profile with just one lock strip cavity as per the plan drawn by Serge Binotto at the Atelier Prouvé (left). The prototypes of that version sent to the construction site turned out to be unusable.

The wider neoprene profile with two lock strip cavities actually used in 1967 (right). The lips of this second version seal better against the glass; the second lock strip, moreover, provides greater protection against break-ins.

The insertion of the large panes called for four people performing a perfectly coordinated series of operations. As the panes selected were the largest possible—if only for aesthetic reasons, as at the time of building—even the tiniest wrong move might result in breakage. After glazing, the lock strips were inserted using a special tool. The photo above shows the sealing profile being slid into place from left to right.

The automotive industry generally gives preference to rounded corners. The mitered corners of the pavilion's window seals were fraught with problems right from the start. Once a pane had been replaced, for example, they could no longer be cleanly resealed, which is why water often seeped into those places. The new silicone seals are relatively easy to glue along the mitered joint. The photos on the right show the mitered joint before and after sealing.

Aluminum foil serving as a separation layer between the vapor barrier and the oak plywood.

Boos & Hahn inspection label, dated November 11, 1966.

Exposure of the enameled panels close to the ground in the studio. Condensation and/or seepage had soaked the insulation material and destroyed the plywood cladding. The new cladding was varnished in the tone of the original, while the varnish on the original panels was merely freshened up.

Dampfsperre
Vapor barrier
Wärmedämmung (Mineralwolle)
Thermal insulation (mineral wool)
Stabilisator (Gips)
Stabilizer (plaster)
Geistlich
geistlich.com

For conservational reasons and in view of the inadequate thermal insulation of the façades, the underfloor heating on the ground floor and the convectors in the upper story were not replaced. One consequence of this is that the pavilion cannot be operated in winter.
It was nevertheless essential that the climatic conditions in the basement be improved, not least to eliminate condensation in the summer. This was achieved with new underfloor heating using thin plastic pipes. The difference in level between the existing concrete plate and the finished slate floor was eliminated by manually sanding down the layer of thermal insulation (foam glass).

The boiler room after restoration. The red, oil-fired boiler was left in situ, complete with the defective feed and return pipes. The new wall-mounted gas boiler is integrated in the existing system.

The new basement heating system consisting of 22 underfloor circuits.

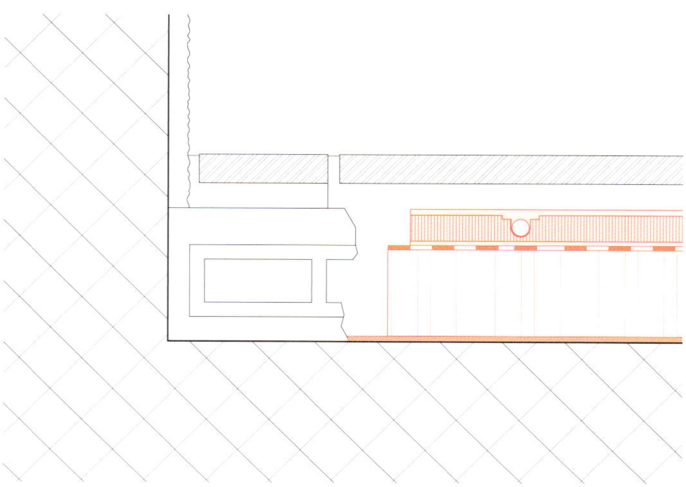

The edge stones of the slate floor were not removed, but left in situ to serve as a reference for the level of the relaid flagstones and for the look of the grouting.

Section through the floor of the basement with the new underfloor heating.

The 20-mm-thick slate flagstones were removed, numbered, and relaid, each in its original position. Only three of the 500 original flagstones had to be replaced.

The original fittings in the secretary's office and the switch cabinet with sliding door after restoration, 2019.

Before restoration
A single glimpse at the switch panel is enough to give us an inkling of the hours of work required to allocate the numerous severed high- and low-voltage lines to all the various contact points, including power outlets, light fixtures, telephone jacks, and burglar alarms. Once identified, each individual line had to be checked and its insulation resistance measured. Practically all the wiring was still intact—which is just as well, since it would not have been possible to thread new cables into the concreted-over installation ducts.

Ramp with its original Pirelli Studway flooring; wall light fixtures after restoration.

All the defective and severely rusted light fixtures—here one from the ramp—had to be replaced with replicas and furnished with new connecting cables; the 220-V lighting and the integrated 12-V emergency lighting were replaced. At least the original cast-glass covers could still be used.

Objets-types

Replicas of the two *tables salon* that Heidi Weber had made after a plan by the Atelier Le Corbusier of July 2, 1959 (FLC 24090). The solid oak slabs are oiled; the leg assembly is made of flat wrought iron.

Sketches and photographs of the tiered seating for the basement, 2016.

Replica corner bench and *tables salon* made with tree slabs.

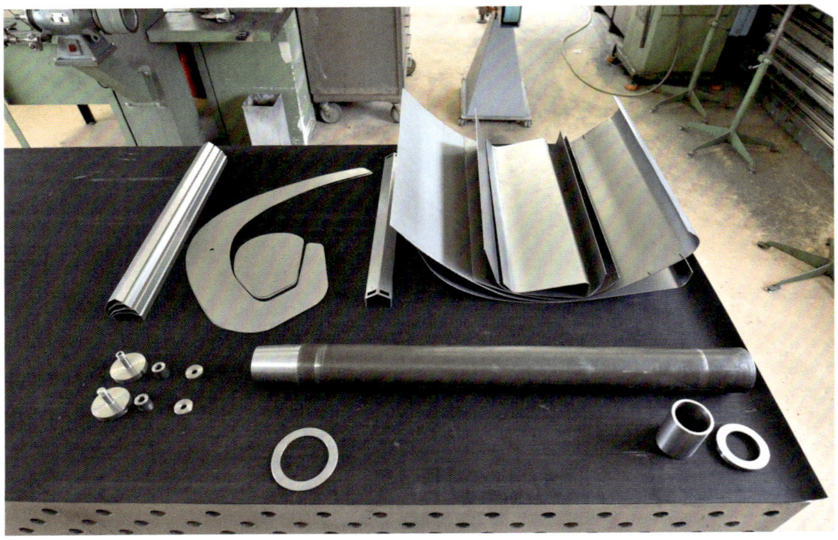

Replica of the type LC I free-standing lamp. Designed in 1951/52, this model was first used in the Unité d'habitation in Marseille.

The replica profile of the lamp holder is made of two bent pieces of sheet metal. The 1.5 mm-thick sheet metal used for the reflector corpus was bent by hand and then welded together.

Replicas of the LC I lamp, the benches, and the wooden cladding in the studio, 2019

Replica of the spotlights (one of 75)
The adapters were found in the U.S.A.; the housing for the E27 fittings and the adapter bracket were reconstructed in Switzerland. The color is based on the few originals to have survived.

Replica of the type LC II "gutter" lamp
The rounded shape, as on the original, was obtained by bending the thin sheet metal in stages. The brackets are made of two welded iron profiles. Each lamp has two E27 fittings. The outside of the housing was spray-painted in black, the inside in white.

Project Organization Restoration 2016–2019

Owner
City of Zurich, Property Management Office (IMMO)

Client's Representative
City of Zurich, Building Surveyor's Office (AHB)

User's Representative
City of Zurich, Cultural Affairs (KTR)

Steering Committee
Peter Haerle, KTR
Wiebke Rösler Häfliger, AHB
Daniel Riedmann, IMMO
Andrea Töndury, Legal Consultant
Martina Glaser, PSS
Peter Baumgartner, Roger Strub,
Department of Preservation of Historical Buildings (KDP)

Preservation of Historical Buildings
Building Department of the Canton of Zurich
Office for Spacial Development
Department of Preservation of Historical Buildings
and Archeological Sites and Monuments

Comité scientifique (advisory board)
Peter Baumgartner, Roger Strub, KDP
Uta Hassler, ETH Zurich
Bénédicte Gandini, Fondation Le Corbusier, Paris
Catherine Dumont d'Ayot, ETH Zurich
Bruno Reichlin, USI Mendrisio

Project Team
Michel Rappaport, Gabriela Kägi Vetter, AHB
Manuel Humbel, IMMO
Alex Schilling, KTR
Lukas Knörr, KDP

Architects and Construction Management
Silvio Schmed and Arthur Rüegg, Zurich

Assistants
Thomas Seiler, Peter Jösler

Civil Engineering
Dr. Deuring + Oehninger AG, Winterthur
Bastian Leu, Martin Deuring

Electrical Engineering
Riesen Elektroplanung GmbH, Zurich
Peter Riesen

HVAC Engineering
Meierhans + Partner AG, Schwerzenbach
Michael Kriegers

Plumbing
Polke, Ziege, von Moos, Zurich
Martin Schultze

Structural Physics
Zehnder & Kälin AG, Winterthur
Richard Zehnder

Landscaping
SKK Landschaftsarchitekten AG, Wettingen
Petra Schröder, Borries Säger

Conservators
Heinz Schwarz & Gertrud Fehringer, Kriens

Timeline	
City Council resolution	June 2016
Construction commenced	September 2017
Completion	March 2019

Statistics	
Built-up volume	2114 m^3 to SIA 416
Floor area	696 m^2
Building costs BKP 0-9	5 million Swiss francs

We would like to thank the businesses and institutions involved in this project for their generous support of this publication:

City of Zurich, Building Surveyor's Office
Client's Representative

Building Department of the Canton of Zurich
Office for Spacial Development
Department of Preservation of Historical Buildings and Archeological Sites and Monuments
Preservation of Historical Buildings

Dr. Deuring + Oehninger AG
Dipl. Bauingenieure ETH SIA USIC, 8401 Winterthur
Seismic safety, corrosion protection

TEKO AG, 6454 Flüelen
Pollutant removal / corrosion protection

Fontana & Fontana AG, 8645 Rapperswil-Jona
Painting and restoration work

Haller Gerüstbau AG, 5615 Fahrwangen
Scaffolding

Omrea AG, 8032 Zurich
Furniture supplies

Prolux Licht AG, 8952 Schlieren
Replica light fixtures

DS-Abdichtungen AG, 8212 Neuhausen
Flat roofwork

Arnet & Co. AG, 8003 Zurich
Natural and artificial stonework

Krapf AG, 9032 Engelburg
Glazing with rubber seals

SIKA Schweiz AG, 8048 Zurich
Paint supplier

KABE Farben, Karl Bubendorf AG, 9001 Gossau
Paint supplier

Meier + Marti GmbH, 8105 Watt-Regensdorf
Sheet metalwork

Raumbau AG, 8005 Zurich
Metal construction work

Kristensen Kittfugen, 5524 Niederwil
Special insulation

A. Grünenwald AG, 8154 Oberglatt
Replica furnishings

W. und R. Rohrer Schlosserei, 8404 Winterthur
Replica studio light fixture

M. Dietiker AG, 8600 Dübendorf
Rubber flooring

Oliver Grüebler, 8038 Zurich
Electrical installations

M. Renggli, 6052 Hergiswil
Surface finishing and conservation work

Meier-Ehrensperger AG, 8047 Zurich
Rendering, concrete repairs

Project Organization 1960–1967

Client
Heidi Weber, Zurich

Architect
Le Corbusier, Paris

Assistants at the Atelier Le Corbusier
Guillermo Jullian de la Fuente,
José Oubrerie, Paris, 1961–1966

Site Architect
Willy Boesiger, Zurich, 1961–February 1966

Consultant
Bernhard Hoesli, Zurich, 1966

Execution Planning/General Construction Management
Alain Tavès, Robert Rebutato, Paris, April 1966–May 1967
Lisbeth Sachs, Zurich, May–July 1967

Engineers
Concrete: René Bollinger, Zurich
Steel frame: Louis Fruitet, Paris
Façade studies: Jean Prouvé, Paris

Site Management
Colin Glennie, Zurich, 1966
Ernst Iten, Winterthur, 1966–1967

Companies involved:
Concrete: AG Heinrich Hatt-Haller, Zurich
Metal: Wartmann & Co. AG, Brugg/Zurich
Enamel: Boos & Hahn, Ortenberg (D)
Glass: Grambach & Co. AG, Zurich
Neoprene: Angst & Pfister AG, Zurich
Insulation: Isotech AG, Zürich / Wanner AG, Horgen
Roof insulation: Meynadier & Co. AG, Zurich
Metalwork: F. Seiler und E. Trütsch, Zurich
Slate: Sponagel AG, Zurich/Schlieren
Rubber flooring: Pirelli, Milan
Heating/plumbing: R. Straessle & Co., Zurich
Wiring: Frick & Co, Zurich / Siemens AG, Zurich
Carpentry: E. Wäspi, Oberstammheim
Painter: Armin Hunziker, Zurich
Lighting: Regent-Intespan, Basel/Zurich

Chronology

April 11 / September 14, 1960
LC views the site in Zurich / accepts the commission
Boesiger is selected as site architect.
June 23, 1960
Zurich City Council approves the use of the site on a fifty-year lease
November 24, 1960
LC in Zurich; meets representatives of the City Council on site
July/August 1961
LC produces twenty-three sketches in his Cabanon on Cap-Martin
September 25, 1961
Collaboration with Louis Fruitet begins
December 29, 1961
Submission of ten plans for the first building permit (the "concrete project")
February 15 / April 13, 1962
First building permit filed / approved
September 18, 1963
Ratification of the fifty-year lease of May 29, 1963
Spring 1964
Construction commences at Höschgasse 8, Zurich
July 28, 1964
New set of plans sent to Boesiger
July 31 / September 18, 1964
Second building permit filed / approved
February 10, 1965
Completion of the double-shell basement
June / July 23, 1965
Set of execution plans completed / validated by LC
August 27, 1965
Death of Le Corbusier at Roquebrune-Cap-Martin
Winter/spring 1965/66 / May 25, 1966
Manufacture, assembly, and erection of the canopies
from April 1966
Execution plans by Tavès and Rebutato
Summer–autumn 1966
Assembly of steel frame, Installation of underfloor heating
Winter 1966/67
Installation of the enameled sheet metal panels
Spring 1967
Installation of the glass panels, then the interior fittings
Early summer 1967 / July 15, 1967
Work on the grounds, pond / inauguration

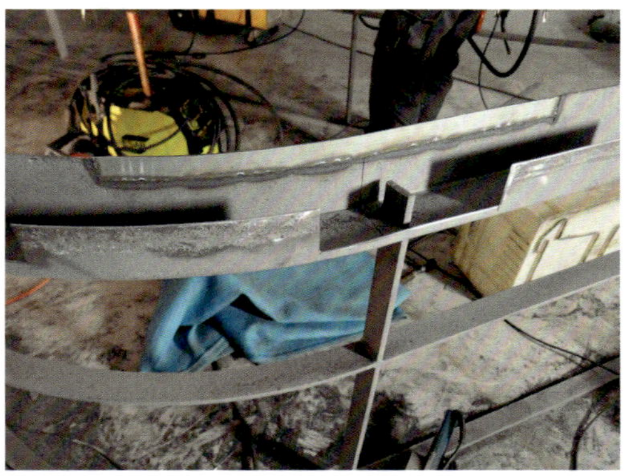

Captions for the whole-page illustrations

Pages 8/9
Rooftop terrace after restoration, 2019
Page 11
"6-Day-Long Zürcher Manifest," September 4–9, 1968 at the Centre Le Corbusier. The painter Gottfried Honegger during a discussion marathon on the ground floor of the pavilion. After the "Globus Riot" of June 1968, twenty-one representatives of the city's cultural, political, and academic establishment sided with the young protesters, forming a working group that soon attracted new members. The Centre Le Corbusier
offered them a forum where participants could share their views on various subjects, including with wall newspapers and placards.
Page 17
Mounting of the canopies, spring 1966
Page 29
Entrance viewed from the inside out, after restoration, 2019
Page 33
New path leading to the Atelier Haller and the Pavillon Le Corbusier, 2019. The path follows the route envisaged in Le Corbusier's original plan.
Pages 38/39
North façade after restoration, 2019
Pages 40/41
East façade with original glazing after restoration, 2019
Pages 42/43
South façade with new sun protection glass after restoration, 2019
Pages 60/61
Section of the south façade after restoration, 2019
Pages 72/73
First floor with view of the park, 2019. As on the ground floor, the inside surfaces have survived by and large in their original state. The old paintwork has been freshened up and the gaps patched over and retouched. The steel frame's gray-and-white coating has been left untouched.
Pages 74/75
The basement with replica of the tiered seating. The false walls made of wood composite board with rear ventilation have higher surface temperatures than the concrete structure underneath. Opening exhibition *Mon univers*, 2019.
Pages 82/83
View of the kitchen and dining area after reconstruction of its state as per 1967. The light fixture is a replica and the kitchen fittings, which match the originals, a find from the site storage area. The table that Tavès and Rebutato modeled on the original in Le Corbusier's own apartment was replaced by one made by Cassina S.p.A. (Model LC 11 P with a top made of Bianco-di-Carrara marble). The bentwood chairs are originals from the 1960s made by horgenglarus; the vase is by Alvar Aalto (Ittala Model 3031). The light-blue wall panel was left in situ as evidence of the many doublings that over the years concealed the oak panels.
Page 88
View of the inside façade of the studio, 2019. All the surfaces are in their original state, barring minimal changes. At least in the upper story, the chimney still has its original coat of red paint.

Notes

The authoritative monographs are: Catherine Dumont d'Ayot (with Tim Benton), *Le Corbusier's Pavilion for Zurich. Model and Prototype of an Ideal Exhibition Space, Institute of Historic Building Research and Conservation (IDB), ETH Zurich* / Lars Müller Publishers, 2013; and Naïma Jornod, *La "Maison d'homme" ou "Heidi Weber Museum-Center Le Corbusier." Le dernier testament architectural de Le Corbusier*, Geneva: Editions Slatkine, 2013.

We would like to thank the photographer Jürg Gasser, Zollikon, for his many valuable pointers and assistance throughout.

Heidi Weber's Exhibition "House"

1 In *Le Corbusier et son atelier rue de Sèvres 35. Œuvre complète publiée par W. Boesiger*, Zurich: Les Editions d'Architecture, 1965, p. 24.
2 Heidi Weber, *Dokumentation über das Centre Le Corbusier*, published on its inauguration, Zurich, 1967 p. 3.
3 Heidi Weber, "Brief Talk" held on July 15, 1977 at the opening of the jubilee exhibition *Zürich entdeckt Le Corbusier*, Zurich, p. 3.
4 Heidi Weber, "Forum für Umweltsfragen," invitation to the opening of the exhibition *Zürich? Diagnose und Therapie für eine Stadt. Eine Ausstellung der Studiengruppe "Bauen für Zeitgenossen,"* February 26, 1970. Margit Staber had hoped for a "study center for the wider field of environmental design" that would extend beyond a mere "memorial to a great man" as early as 1967, cf. idem, "Das neue Le Corbusier-Zentrum in Zürich," in *Süddeutsche Zeitung*, September 27, 1967, n.p.
5 Heidi Weber moved her own business premises to Willy Boesiger's "Select-Haus" at Limmatquai 16.
6 New name introduced on the tenth anniversary in 1977.

The Realization of a Manifesto

1 Stanislaus von Moos, "Der Corbusier-Pavillon. Ein Bau von Le Corbusier in Zürich," in *Neue Zürcher Zeitung*, No. 192, July 15, 1967, p. 13.
2 Descriptions after v.S., "Centre Le Corbusier Heidi Weber Zürich," in *Baumeister, Zeitschrift für Architektur, Planung, Umwelt*, 1967/11, pp. 1383–1390.
3 Conversations with Serge Binotto on June 13, 2015 and Robert Rebutato on June 19, 2015.
4 Heinz Ronner, "Le Corbusier: Material und Technik. Das Eisen und der Pavillon in Zürich," in Anne-Marie Disserens et al. (eds.), *Heinz Ronner*, Zurich: ETH, Chair of Heinz Ronner, 1991, p. 95.

Le Corbusier's Last Work

1 Catherine Dumont d'Ayot (with Tim Benton), *Le Corbusiers Pavillon für Zürich. Modell und Prototyp eines idealen Ausstellungsraums*, op. cit.
2 Planungs- und Baugesetz (PBG) (Planning and Building Law) of Canton Zurich of September 7, 1975, § 204.

Restoration, Reconstruction, Retrofitting

1 The replicas of the missing furnishings and fittings expeditiously made in 2016 were marked with gray paint to tell them apart from the originals.

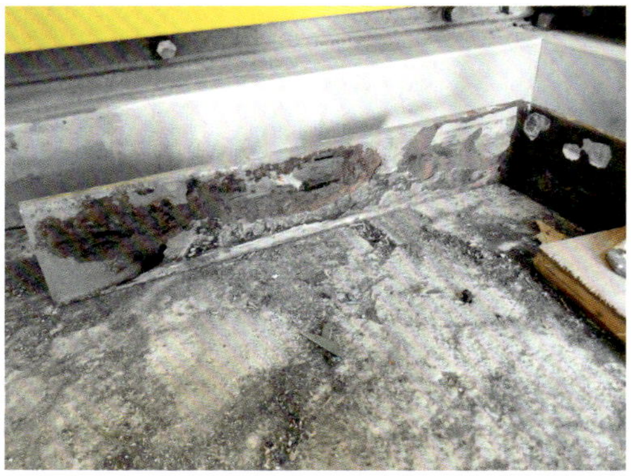

View of the construction site, summer 1966
The steel frame being assembled; in the foreground the ramp with the demolished end wall.
The gondola ropeway has already been taken down.